# AWESOME JOKES

FOR   YEAR OLDS

## SILLY JOKES FOR KIDS AGED 5

# What do you call a boy lying on your porch?

*a. Matt.*

# What does a squirrel say when she's done praying?

*a. "Almond!"*

# Knock knock.
*a. Who's there?*
## b. Boo.
*c. Boo who?*
## d. Don't cry! It's only a joke.

# Where do berries sit?

*a. In a chairy.*

# What do you call a naughty sheep.

*a. Baaaaaaad.*

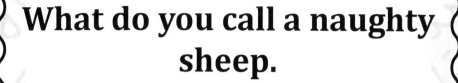

# What kind of animal do you look like when you get out of the shower?

*a. A little bear.*

# What does a seal have over his floor?

*a. A sealing.*

# What is green and smells like purple paint?

*a. Green paint.*

# What did the gardener put in his cake batter?

*a. A cup of flower.*

# What did the cap say to the scarf?

*a. "You can hang around while I go on a head."*

# Knock knock.

*a. Who's there?*
*b. Cash.*
*c. Cash who?*
*d. No thank you, I prefer almonds.*

# Where do flowers go to learn?

*a. Kindergarden.*

# What do ghosts say when they're sad?

*a. BOO hoo.*

# What do you give your sneaker when it sneezes?

*a. A tiSHOE.*

# What do you call your dad with socks in his ears?

*a. Anything you want, he can't hear you.*

# What kind of shoes to spies wear?

*a. Sneakers.*

# What's the best day to go to McDonald's?

*a. On Fry-day.*

# What do you call a fish without any eyes?

*a. A fsh.*

# What is an owl's favorite game?

*a. Guess WHO.*

## Knock knock.

*a. Who's there?*
**b. Tank.**

*c. Tank who?*
**d. You're welcome!**

# What is the best game to play in the ocean?

*a. Tide and seek.*

# What goes "ha ha ha THUMP"?

*a. Someone laughing their head off.*

# What kind of food do you get out of your nose?

*a. A hambooger.*

# Where should you store your toothpaste?

*a. In the basemint.*

# What do you call a boomerang that won't come back?

*a. A banana.*

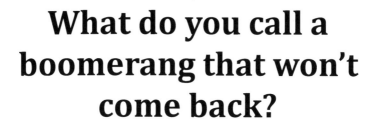

# What kind of keys don't open doors?

*a. Monkeys and donkeys.*

# What did the eyeball say to his neighbor?

*a. Just between us, something smells.*

# What do you have when you've got a broken down car and a dead cell phone?

*a. Bad luck.*

# What do you call someone who protects windows?

*a. A screensaver.*

## Knock knock.

*a. Who's there?*
**b. Cargo.**

*c. Cargo who?*
**d. Cargo VROOM!**

# Knock knock.

*a. Who's there?*
**b. Luke.**

*c. Luke who?*
**d. Luke out behind you.**

# What goes "tick, bark, tock, bark, tick, bark, tock"?

*a. A watchdog.*

# Why does a robin carry a worm in its beak?

*a. Because it doesn't have any pockets.*

# What do you call a pirate painter?

*a. An arrrrrtist.*

# What do cats eat for dessert on a cold day?

*a. Mice cream.*

# What do you call two banana peels?

*a. A pair of slippers.*

# What kind of fruit do you always have two of?

*a. A pear.*

# Why are elephants the best swimmers?

*a. Because they have trunks.*

# What flies and goes on toast?

*a. A jellycopter.*

# Where do fish go to get money?

*a. To the river bank.*

# What do big whales eat?

*a. Fish and chips.*

# Where do you take an injured horse?

*a. To the horse-pital.*

# Knock knock.

*a. Who's there?*
**b. Beats.**

*c. Beats who?*
**d. Beats me.**

# Why do bees have the best hair?

*a. Because they have combs.*

# Knock knock.

*a. Who's there?*
*b. Beef.*
*c. Beef who?*
*d. Let me in beef-ore I catch a cold.*

# Knock knock.

*a. Who's there?*
**b. Kiwi.**

*c. Kiwi who?*
**d. Kiwi go soon please?**

# Knock knock.

*a. Who's there?*
*b. Turnip.*
*c. Turnip who?*
*d. Turnip the volume,*
   *I can't hear.*

# Knock knock.

*a. Who's there?*
*b. Doughnut.*
*c. Doughnut who?*
*d. Doughnut tell anyone, it's*
   *a secret.*

# Knock knock.

*Who's there?*
**Abe.**

*Abe who?*
**Now I know my Abe B C's.**

# Knock knock.

*a. Who's there?*
**b. Ada.**

*c. Ada who?*
**d. Ada lot to eat today.**

**Knock knock.**

*Who's there?*
**Alex.**
*Alex who?*
**Alex the questions
here, alright.**

**Knock knock.**

*a. Who's there?*
**b. Amy.**

*c. Amy who?*
**d. Amy fraid I can't tell you.**

# Knock knock.

*a. Who's there?*

**b. Anita.**

*c. Anita who?*

**d. Anita borrow a cup of sugar.**

# Knock knock.

*a. Who's there?*

**b. Annie.**

*c. Annie who?*

**d. Annie body home?**

# Knock knock.

*a. Who's there?*
**b. Barbie.**

*c. Barbie who?*
**d. Fire up the Barbie cue!**

# Knock knock.

*a. Who's there?*
**b. Ben.**
*c. Ben who?*
**d. Ben here for hours,
let me in!**

# Knock knock.

*a. Who's there?*

**b. Doris.**

*c. Doris who?*

**d. Doris still closed. Let me in!**

# Knock knock.

*a. Who's there?*

**b. Frank.**

*c. Frank who?*

**d. Frank you for inviting me over!**

# Knock knock.

*a. Who's there?*

## b. Ken.

*c. Ken who?*

## d. Ken I come in, I've been waiting forever.

# What is the saddest kind of bird?

*a. A blue jay.*

# What do you call a dog who isn't smooth?

*a. Ruff.*

# What kind of music do rabbits listen to?

*a. Hip hop.*

# What do you call a cow who can't give milk?

*a. A milk dud.*

# What kind of hair do mermaids have?

*a. Wavy.*

# How does a fish weigh itself?

*a. With a scale.*

# What do you call a bear who lost all its teeth?

*a. A gummy bear.*

# What do you call a napping cow?

*a. A bulldozer.*

# What did the cat say to the mouse?

*a. "Please to eat you."*

# What is a dog's least favorite place to buy things?

## *a. The flea market.*

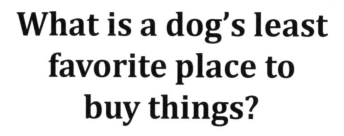

# What kind of fish comes out at night?

## *a. A starfish.*

# What is a scientist's favorite kind of clothes?

*a. Genes.*

# What does Mickey Mouse drive?

*a. A Minnie van.*

# Why did the man wear sneakers to bed?

*a. So he could catch up on sleep.*

# What's it called when a dinosaur crashes his truck?

*a. Tyrannosaurus wrecks.*

# What do birds say on Halloween?

*a. Trick or tweet.*

# Wear do kindergarten cows eat their lunch?

*a. In the calf-eteria.*

# What did the spider wear to her wedding?

*a. A webbing dress.*

# What did the firefighter name his sons?

*a. José and Hose B.*

# Why can't you trust a pig?

*a. Because they squeal.*

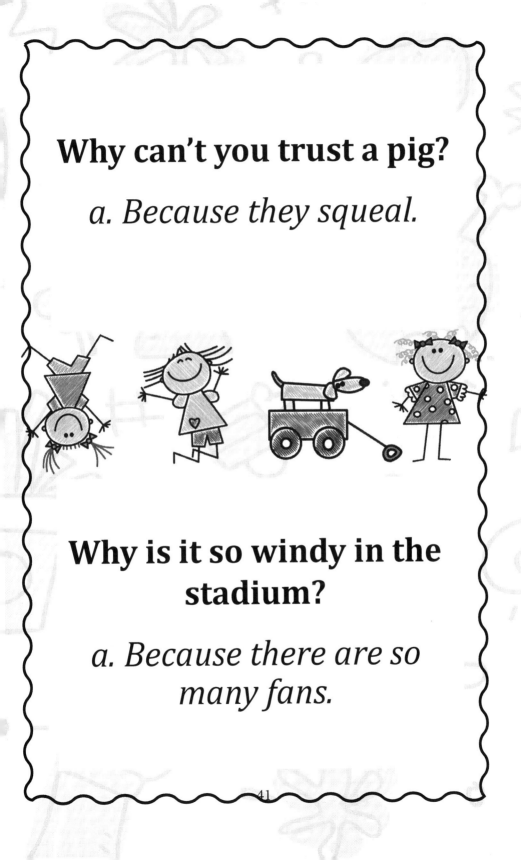

# Why is it so windy in the stadium?

*a. Because there are so many fans.*

# Knock knock.

*a. Who's there?*
**b. Stopwatch.**

*c. Stopwatch who?*
**d. Stopwatch you're doing so you can let me in.**

**Why did the mushroom have so many friends?**

*a. Because he was a fun guy.*

# What do polar bears wear to baseball games?

*a. Ice caps.*

# What did the alien say to the bird?

*a. Take me to your tweeter.*

# What was the little monster's favorite thing to play?

*a. Swallow the leader.*

# How do you make a burger when you're in the jungle?

*a. Put it on the grilla.*

# What do you call a fairy who never takes a bath?

*a. Stinkerbell.*

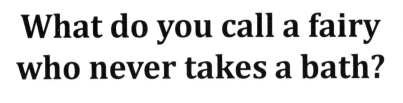

# What is a fly without any wings called?

*a. A walk.*

# What magical person grants you fishes?

*a. The fairy codmother.*

## Knock knock.

*a. Who's there.*
**b. Amish.**

*c. Amish who?*
**d. Amish you so much!**

**Knock knock.**
*a. Who's there?*
**b. Yukon.**

*c. Yukon who?*
**d. Yukon let me in and find out!**

**Knock knock.**
*a. Who's there?*
**b. Honey bee.**
*c. Honey bee who?*
**d. Honey bee a darling and open the door?**

# Knock knock.
*a. Who's there?*
## b. Goat.
*c. Goat who?*
## d. Goat to the window and see.

# Knock knock.
*a. Who's there?*
## b. Will.
*c. Will who?*
## d. Will you please let me in already?

**Knock knock.**
*a. Who's there?*
**b. Wendy.**
*c. Wendy who?*
**d. Wendy bell is fixed I won't have to knock anymore.**

**Knock knock.**
*a. Who's there?*
**b. Tyrone.**
*c. Tyrone who?*
**d. Tyrone tie, you're an adult!**

**Knock knock.**
*a. Who's there?*
**b. Sherlock.**
*c. Sherlock who?*
**d. Sherlock your door every night, don't you.**

**Knock knock.**
*a. Who's there?*
**b. Otto.**
*c. Otto who?*
**d. Otto know by the sound of my voice.**

**Knock knock.**
*a. Who's there?*
**b. Lena.**
*c. Lena who?*
**d. Lena little closer so you can hear me.**

**Knock knock.**
*a. Who's there.*
**b. Kent.**
*c. Kent who?*
**d. Kent you just let me in already?**

Made in the USA
Las Vegas, NV
16 March 2023

69163509R00028